A Beginner's Guide To THE PLANT BASED DIET

Over 150 Awesome Plant-Based Recipe for a Healthy and Balanced Diet.

| June 2021 Edition |

© **Copyright 2021 by Irene Milani**

Table of Contents

Introduction 1

Plant Based Diet Food List 4

Chapter 1: Breakfast and Smoothies 6

    Chia Berries Smoothie 6

    Cucumber Avocado Smoothie 8

    Hot Pink Smoothie 9

    Maca Caramel Smoothie 11

    Tofu Detox Smoothie 13

    Maple Blueberry Shake 15

    Valentine Smoothie 16

    Pina Colada Smoothie 18

    Vegan Breakfast Sandwich 19

    Greek Chickpeas Toast 22

    Tofu Pancakes 24

    Waffles with Blueberry Sauce 27

    Jam Cheese Sandwich 30

Chapter 2: Delicious Main Dish Recipes for Lunch. 32

    Banh Mi 32

    Sweet Potato Buddha Bowl Almond Butter Dressing 34

    Curry Spiced Sweet Potato Wild Rice Burgers 38

    Calabacitas Quesadillas 40

    Chickpea Avocado Salad Sandwich With Cranberries 42

    Rice Paper Rolls with Mango and Mint 44

Turmeric Chickpea Salad Sandwich...47

Mexican Quinoa 48

Potato Fritters 50

Tempeh Reuben 53

Broccoli Pesto with Pasta and Cherry Tomatoes.............................56

Korean Barbecue Tempeh Wraps...58

Crab Cakes 61

Smoky Black Beans Parsley Chimichurri 64

Tuna Sandwich With Chickpeas 67

Sweet Potato Toast 69

Chickpeas with Dates, Turmeric, Cinnamon and Almonds..............71

Cucumber Avocado Toast 73

Tofu Fish Sticks...75

Cornmeal Breaded Tofu 77

Baked Sweet Potato Fries 79

Wheat Thins...81

Spinach and Artichoke Dip...83

Coconut Bacon 85

Chapter 3: Delicious Main Dish Recipes for Dinner. 88

Brown Rice Stir Fry with Vegetables...88

Grilled Veggie Skewers...90

Eggplant Teriyaki Bowls 92

Quinoa and Black Bean Chilli 95

Mac and Cheese...97

Butternut Squash Linguine With Fried Sage 100

Paella 102

Spicy Thai Peanut Sauce Over Roasted Sweet Potatoes and Rice . 105

Butternut Squash Chipotle Chili With Avocado............................... 108

Chickpea Biryani 111

Chinese Eggplant.. 114

Black Pepper Tofu with Bok Choy.. 117

Spaghetti Alla Puttanesca... 119

Thai Red Curry.. 121

Thai Green Curry with Spring Vegetables 123

Tamarind Potato Curry... 125

West African Stew with Sweet Potato and Greens........................ 127

Kale Slaw 129

Chapter 4: Soups and Salads..131

Moroccan Veggie Soup 131

Tex Mex Black Bean and Avocado Salad.................................... 133

Lentil Fattoush Salad.. 135

Sweet Potato Salad 137

Lentil Salad with Spinach and Pomegranate............................... 139

Broccoli Salad Curry Dressing.. 142

Broccoli Cauliflower Soup... 143

Carrot Ginger Soup 145

Persimmon Butternut Squash Soup 147

Eggplant Tomato Soup 149

Black Bean Soup 151

Chapter 5: Desserts and Snacks 153

Vegan Chocolate 153

Peanut Butter Cup Cookies.. 155

Lemon Tarts...157

Peanut Butter Caramel Rice Krispies.......................................159

Vanilla Macaroons 161

Carrot Cake 163

Pumpkin Pie 166

Chapter 6: Drinks...169

Gingerbread Latte..169

Black Forest Shake...171

Turmeric Lassi..173

Pumpkin Spice Turmeric Latte 174

Mexican Hot Chocolate 175

Coconut Cream Shake 177

Lemon Ginger Detox Tea 178

Carrot Pineapple Ginger Juice 179

Strawberry Shrub Mocktail 180

Strawberry Margaritas 182

Fresh Mint Julep..183

30-Days Meal Plan...186

Day 1 186

Day 2 186

Day 3 186

Day 4 186

Day 5 187

Day 6 187

Day 7 187

Day 8 188

Day 9 188

Day 10 188

Day 11 189

Day 12 189

Day 13 189

Day 14 190

Day 15 190

Day 16 190

Day 17 191

Day 18 191

Day 19 191

Day 20 192

Day 21 192

Day 22 192

Day 23 192

Day 24 193

Day 25 193

Day 26 193

Day 27 194

Day 28 194

Day 29 194

Day 30 195

Conclusion 196

Legal & Disclaimer

The information contained in this book and its contents is not designed to replace or take the place of any form of medical or professional advice; and is not meant to replace the need for independent medical, financial, legal or other professional advice or services, as may be required. The content and information in this book have been provided for educational and entertainment purposes only.

The content and information contained in this book has been compiled from sources deemed reliable, and it is accurate to the best of the Author's knowledge, information and belief. However, the Author cannot guarantee its accuracy and validity and cannot be held liable for any errors and/or omissions. Further, changes are periodically made to this book as and when needed. Where appropriate and/or necessary, you must consult a professional (including but not limited to your doctor, attorney, financial advisor or such other professional advisor) before using any of the suggested remedies, techniques, or information in this book.

Upon using the contents and information contained in this book, you agree to hold harmless the Author from and against any damages, costs, and expenses, including any legal fees potentially resulting from the application of any of the information provided by this book. This disclaimer applies to any loss, damages or injury caused by the use and application, whether directly or indirectly, of any advice or information presented, whether for breach of contract, tort, negligence, personal injury, criminal intent, or under any other cause of action.

You agree to accept all risks of using the information presented inside this book.

You agree that by continuing to read this book, where appropriate and/or necessary, you shall consult a professional (including but not limited to your doctor, attorney, or financial advisor or such other advisor as needed) before using any of the suggested remedies, techniques, or information in this book.

Introduction

Plant-based diets are becoming widely popular and more and more people are switching to plant-based diets for a variety of reasons. Diets that are based on consumption of plant foods and are rich in beans, nuts, seeds, fruit and vegetables, whole grains, and cereal based foods can provide all the nutrients needed for good health and offer affordable, tasty and nutritious alternatives to meat-based diets.

A plant-based diet means eating foods that mostly or entirely made from plants, and it actually allows you meet your nutritional needs by consuming foods in which none or close to none of the ingredients come from animals. A plant-based diet also focuses on healthful whole foods, rather than processed foods.

Plant based diet is rich in nutrients, and if you go from a Western diet to a plant based one, you will stop eating animal products and switch to plant based foods you will start getting more fiber, antioxidants, beneficial plant compounds, potassium, magnesium, folate and vitamins A, C and E, which in result will improve your health. But this type of diet should be carefully planned to achieve that desired result.

Plant based diet may lower the risk of cancer and people on vegan diet may have a 15% lower risk of getting cancer or die from it. It can be effective at reducing symptoms of arthritis such as pain, joint swelling and morning stiffness.

Plant based diet can also help with losing weight. Several trusted studies show that this kind of diet is more efficient when compared with other weight loss diets. As a result, vegans tend to be thinner and have lower body mass indexes (BMIs) than non-vegans.

The diet also improves kidney function and reduces the risk of poor performance. It can even help with reducing the risk of developing Alzheimer's disease.

In this book you will find delicious and simple plant-based recipes that will be suitable even for those who only start their Plant Based journey. All the recipes are divided into sections:

➢ *Breakfast and Smoothies*
➢ *Recipes for Lunch*
➢ *Recipes for Dinner*
➢ *Soups and Salads*
➢ *Desserts and Snacks*
➢ *Drinks*
➢ *30-Days Meal Plan*

In addition, you will find 30 Days Meal Plan with the best recipes that you can cook in no time. With this book your transition to the Plant Based Diet will be smooth and you and your family will not even notice it!

Plant Based Diet Food List

If you are on a vegan diet you do not have to eat only vegetables and fruits. Lots of usual dishes are already vegan or can be easily turned into vegan. And people that follow the vegan path have a wide variety of options to choose from to substitute animal products.

- Seitan, tempeh and tofu are versatile protein-rich options that can replace meat, poultry fish and eggs.
- Peas, lentils and beans have lots of nutrients and beneficial plant compounds.
- Nuts are a perfect choice in terms of fiber, iron, zinc,
- magnesium, vitamin E and selenium.
- Chia, flaxseeds and hemp seeds contain omega-3 fatty acids, and protein.
- Plant milks and yogurts help achieve the needed daily calcium intakes.
- Chlorella and spirulina have complete protein in them, while other varieties of algae have iodine.
- Nutritional yeast has protein in it.
- The whole family of whole grains, cereals can help with complex carbohydrates, fiber, iron, B vitamins and various minerals. To get as much protein as possible choose spelt, teff, amaranth and quinoa.
- Fruits and vegetables are great choices to increase the nutrient intake.

People that switched to plant-based diet must **avoid** consuming any animal products and products that have ingredients of animal origin.

- Meat, poultry and products that contain any meat ingredients.
- Fish, seafood and products that contain any seafood ingredients.
- Dairy and products that contain any dairy ingredients.
- Eggs and products that contain any egg ingredients.

Chapter 1: Breakfast and Smoothies

Chia Berries Smoothie

Cooking time: 5 minutes

Servings: 2

Ingredients

- 1 cup raspberries, frozen
- 1 teaspoon ground cardamom
- 1 1/2 cups almond milk
- 1/2 cup strawberries, frozen
- 3 tablespoons chia seeds

Instructions

1. Add a cup of almond milk into a bowl along with the chia seeds, and then allow to rest for about an hour, until the chia seeds have expanded, and the desired texture turns pudding like.

2. Put the chia mixture into the blender along with the remaining almond milk, cardamom and the frozen berries. Blitz until combined and smooth.

3. Pour into chilled glasses and serve.

Cucumber Avocado Smoothie

Cooking time: 5 minutes

Servings: 2

Ingredients

- 1/2 small cucumber
- 1/2 cup almond milk
- 2 handfuls fresh baby spinach
- 1 lemon juiced
- 1/2 avocado

Instructions

1. Add all the ingredients for the smoothie to a blender. Blitz until combined and smooth.

2. Pour into chilled glasses and serve.

Hot Pink Smoothie

Cooking time: 5 minutes

Servings: 2

Ingredients

- ½ cup red berries
- ¼ teaspoon vanilla extract
- 1 clementine or tangerine, peeled, chopped
- 1 tablespoon chia seeds
- ½ ripe banana, fresh or frozen
- 2 tablespoons unsalted almond butter, raw or roasted
- 1 small beet, peeled, chopped
- 2 tablespoons unsalted almond butter, raw or roasted
- 1 cup almond milk
- Salt, to taste

Instructions

1. Add all the ingredients for the smoothie to a blender. Blitz until combined and smooth.

2. Pour into chilled glasses and serve.

Maca Caramel Smoothie

Cooking time: 5 minutes

Servings: 2

Ingredients

- 2 soft Medjool dates, pitted
- 1/4 cup cold coffee, brewed
- 1/2 teaspoon vanilla extract
- 1 handful ice cubes

- 1/4 cup raw cashews, soaked (4 hours in cold water or 10 minutes in boiling water)
- 1/2 banana, sliced, frozen
- 1/4 cup milk, plant-based
- 1 teaspoon maca powder
- 1/8 teaspoon salt

Instructions

1. Add all the ingredients for the smoothie to a blender. Blitz until combined and smooth.
2. Pour into chilled glasses and serve.

Tofu Detox Smoothie

Cooking time: 5 minutes

Servings: 2

Ingredients

- 1/2 cup bananas, peeled, sliced, frozen
- 1 cup berries, frozen

- 1 cup organic spinach or kale

- 1 cup fruit juice

- 2 tablespoons silken tofu

- 1 tablespoon flaxseed meal

Instructions

1. Add all the ingredients for the smoothie to a blender. Blitz until combined and smooth.

2. Pour into chilled glasses and serve.

Maple Blueberry Shake

Cooking time: 5 minutes

Servings: 2

Ingredients

- 1/4 cup water

- 1/2 teaspoon maple extract

- 1/2 cup cottage cheese, or low-fat yogurt

- 2 teaspoons flaxseed meal

- 3 tablespoons vanilla protein powder

- 1/2 cup frozen blueberries

- 1/4 teaspoon vanilla extract

- Sweetener, to taste

- 1 handful ice cubes

Instructions

1. Add all the ingredients for the smoothie to a blender. Blitz until combined and smooth.

2. Pour into chilled glasses and serve.

Valentine Smoothie

Cooking time: 5 minutes

Servings: 2

Ingredients

- 2 cups soy milk, chilled
- 2 small figs, fresh
- 1 teaspoon maca powder
- 1 tablespoon maple syrup
- 1/2 teaspoon sweet paprika
- 1/2 cup cashew nuts
- 2 tablespoons raw cacao powder
- 1 cup raspberries, frozen
- fresh raspberries, to serve

Instructions

1. Add all the ingredients for the smoothie to a blender. Blitz until combined and smooth.
2. Pour into chilled glasses and serve topped with fresh raspberries and a sprinkle of cacao powder.

Cooking time: 5 minutes

Servings: 2

Ingredients

- 13.5 oz. coconut milk
- 3 bananas peeled, frozen
- 20 oz. crushed pineapples with juice

Instructions

1. Add all the ingredients for the smoothie to a blender. Blitz until combined and smooth.

2. Pour into chilled glasses and serve.

Vegan Breakfast Sandwich

Cooking time: 15 minutes

Servings: 4

Ingredients

For the tofu:

- 2 tablespoons water
- 2 tablespoons soy sauce
- 1 block extra-firm tofu, pressed, sliced into 4 pieces
- 1/2 teaspoon garlic powder
- 2 tablespoons nutritional yeast
- 2 tablespoons olive oil
- 1 teaspoon liquid smoke
- 1 teaspoon hot sauce

For the sandwich:

- 1 tomato, sliced
- 1 avocado, mashed
- 4 English muffins, halved, toasted

Instructions

1. Prepare the tofu by mixing nutritional yeast together with soy sauce, water, olive oil, liquid smoke, garlic powder and hot sauce in a sealable bag, and then add tofu pieces and shake well until the pieces are evenly coated. Marinate for at least 30 minutes.

2. When done, heat a skillet over medium heat until hot, and then add the coated tofu slices along with the remaining marinade. Cook on each side for about 5 minutes until brown.

3. When done, prepare the vegan sandwich by spreading ¼ of mashed avocado on the English muffin, and then top with a slice of tofu, add 2 slices of tomatoes, and layer another English muffin on top. Repeat the same process with the remaining ingredients until you prepare 4 sandwiches.
4. Serve ad enjoy!

Greek Chickpeas Toast

Cooking time: 15 minutes

Servings: 4

Ingredients

- 2 tablespoons olive oil

- 3 small shallots, diced

- ¼ teaspoon smoked paprika

- ½ teaspoon cinnamon or cumin

- 6 slices crusty bread, toasted

- ½ teaspoon sweet paprika

- 2 large skinned tomatoes, chopped

- 2 large garlic cloves, diced

- Salt, sugar and pepper, taste

- 2 cups chickpeas, cooked

- ¼ handful pitted Kalamata olives, to garnish

- fresh parsley or dill, to garnish

Instructions

1. Add oil to a pan placed over medium heat. When hot, add shallots and fry gently until translucent. Add garlic to the pan and continue frying until softened and the shallots are fully translucent.

2. When done, add all spices into the pan and fry for about 1-2 minutes stirring often.

3. Roughly chop the tomatoes and then add them to the pan along with several tablespoons of water. Simmer on low heat until the sauce is thick.

4. When the sauce has thickened, add the precooked chickpeas and cook for 2-3 minutes. Adjust sugar, salt and pepper to taste.

5. When done, top the toasted bread with chickpeas, black olives and fresh herbs. Enjoy!

Tofu Pancakes

Cooking time: 15 minutes

Servings: 4

Ingredients

- 3 tablespoons brazil nuts
- 1 cups raspberries
- 3 bananas, sliced

- Maple syrup or honey, to serve

For the batter:

- 3 tablespoons vegetable oil
- 14 oz. firm tofu
- 1 tablespoons baking powder
- 1 cup buckwheat flour
- 1½ teaspoons ground mixed spice
- 2 cups almond milk
- 2 teaspoons vanilla extract
- 4 tablespoons light muscovado sugar
- 2 teaspoons lemon juice

Instructions

1. Preheat the oven to 350F and evenly spread the nuts on a baking tray. Allow the nuts to cook for 5 minutes until golden and toasted through. When done, let the nuts cool and then finely chop them.

2. Place the tofu into a bowl along with lemon juice, half of the milk and vanilla, and then blend them together with a blender stick until liquid. Continue blending until the yoghurt-like thickness and smoothness is achieved. When done, stir the liquid into the oil along with the remaining milk in order to allow the mixture to loosen.

3. Add all the dry ingredients into a bowl along with a teaspoon of salt and whisk well until combine and aerate. When done, drill a hole in the middle of the mixture and add the tofu mixture and squeeze together to prepare a batter which is nicely thick.

4. Swirl a tablespoon of oil round a non-stick frying pan over medium heat. When both pan and oil are hot, ladle in 3 spoonful of the batter evenly spread and allow one side to bake for 2 minutes until bubbly over almost all surface and then flip and bake the other side for a single minute until firm and puffed up. When done set the cooked pancakes aside and repeat the same procedure with the remaining batter using less oil each time.

5. When done, serve the warm pancakes along with berries, bananas, toasted nuts and drizzle the top with honey or syrup.

Waffles with Blueberry Sauce

Cooking time: 15 minutes

Servings: 4

Ingredients

For the waffles:

- 1 1/2 tablespoons baking powder
- 1 cup water
- 3 tablespoons canola oil
- 3 tablespoons sugar
- 1/2 teaspoon lemon zest
- 1 teaspoon vanilla extract
- 1/8 teaspoon salt
- 1 1/2 cups white spelt flour
- 2 1/2 tablespoons lemon juice

For the blueberry sauce:

- 1 1/2 cups blueberries, fresh or frozen
- 1 1/2 tablespoons sugar

Instructions

1. Preheat the waffle iron and combine the white spelt flour together with the baking powder, sugar, lemon zest and salt.
2. Add canola oil into the mixture along with vanilla extract, water and lemon juice.
3. Let the batter rest for a few minutes, and then spoon the batter into the preheated waffle iron. Carefully follow the waffle iron instructions and cook the batter accordingly.

4. When done, prepare the sauce by adding the blueberries into a pan along with sugar. Place the pan over medium heat and heat until the berries have softened and all the juices have been released.

5. Taste the sauce and adjust the sugar, and then serve the waffles with blueberry sauce. Enjoy!

Jam Cheese Sandwich

Cooking time: 10 minutes

Servings: 1

Ingredients

- 1 English muffin, toasted
- 1 teaspoon hot sauce
- 1 teaspoon olive oil
- 1 teaspoon strawberry jam
- 1/4 avocado
- 1 vegan cheese slice
- Leafy greens of choice
- 1 vegan sausage patty, crumbled

Instructions

1. Oil the skillet and place over medium heat and then add the patty and cook for a minute, flip it on the other side and add cheese. Cook in the skillet until cheese is melted and then remove from heat.
2. Half the toasted English muffin, add jam and then add patty along with the melted cheese on top.
3. When done, add your favorite leafy greens and avocado, and then serve and enjoy!

Chapter 2: Delicious Main Dish Recipes for Lunch.

Banh Mi

Cooking Time: 20 minutes

Servings: 4

Ingredients

- 1 ½ cup raw vegetables, cabbage and carrots, shredded
- 1 cup hummus
- 8 oz. cooked tempeh, very finely sliced
- 1 long French baguette
- ½ small pack coriander leaves
- ½ small pack mint leaves
- 3 tablespoons white wine vinegar
- 1 teaspoon golden caster sugar
- hot sauce
- salt, to taste

Instructions

1. Place vegetables, vinegar, caster sugar and salt in a large bowl, mix well and set aside to marinate.
2. Heat the oven to 360F.
3. Place baguette in the oven pan, slice it in 4 slices, and cook in the oven for 5 minutes.
4. Once done, remove from the oven, spread hummus on 2 slices, top with 4 tempeh pieces and pickled vegetables.
5. Sprinkle coriander, mint leaves and top with the other 2 remaining baguette slices.

Sweet Potato Buddha Bowl Almond Butter Dressing

Cooking Time: 1 hour

Servings: 4

Ingredients

For the roasted vegetables:

- 1 large head broccoli, cut into florets
- 2 sweet potatoes, cubed
- 2 cloves garlic, minced
- 1 tablespoon toasted sesame oil
- salt and pepper

For the mango coconut rice:

- 2 teaspoons coconut oil
- 1 cup unsweetened coconut milk
- 1 cup water
- 1 cup brown rice, uncooked
- 1 ripe mango, diced

For the almond butter dressing:

- ¼ cup natural creamy almond butter
- 4 tablespoons fresh orange juice
- 2 teaspoons maple syrup
- ½ teaspoon apple cider vinegar
- 1 teaspoon coconut oil, melted

Instructions

1. Place the pot over medium heat, add coconut oil.

2. Add brown rice and cook for 5 minutes, add water and coconut milk and bring it to a boil. Cover, reduce the heat and let it simmer for about 45 minutes.

3. When done add mango, salt, and set aside

4. Preheat the oven 375F and line a baking sheet with parchment paper.

5. Place sweet potatoes in a microwave safe bowl and heat it for about 4 minutes, then transfer to the prepared baking sheet.

6. Add broccoli florets, minced garlic to the baking sheet and mix well.

7. Bake in the oven for 30 minutes until tender.

8. Mix almond butter dressing ingredients in a medium bowl.

9. Serve rice in bowls, top with roasted vegetables and 2 tablespoons of the almond dressing.

Curry Spiced Sweet Potato Wild Rice Burgers

Cooking Time: 1 hour 15 minutes

Servings: 6

Ingredients

- 1 sweet potato
- ½ cup wild rice blend, uncooked
- 15 oz. can chickpeas, rinsed and drained
- ½ cup breadcrumbs
- 1/3 cup dried cranberries
- 2 teaspoons coconut oil
- 1 teaspoon curry powder
- 1 ½ teaspoons cumin
- ¼ teaspoon garlic powder
- salt and pepper

Instructions

1. Prepare a pan with parchment lined paper and preheat the oven to 400F.
2. Place sweet potato on the pan and poke it with a fork. Bake for 45 minutes.
3. Place a small pan over medium heat. Add rice, water and bring to a boil. Cover, reduce the heat and let it simmer for 40 minutes.
4. Place sweet potato and chickpeas in a food processor, process for about 10 seconds and transfer to a large bowl.
5. Add cooked rice, curry powder, cumin, garlic, salt, pepper and mix well.
6. Add breadcrumbs, cranberries, pecans, mix well and scoop the mixture with damp hands and shape them into patties, set aside.
7. Place a large pan over medium heat, add coconut oil.
8. Fry patties in batches once oil is very hot for 8 minutes on each side.

Calabacitas Quesadillas

Cooking Time: 20 minutes

Servings: 2

Ingredients

- 2 large whole wheat tortillas
- ½ cup vegan Mexican shreds
- ½ onion, diced
- 1 jalapeno, seeded and diced
- 1 zucchini, quartered
- kernels from 1 ear of sweet corn
- 1 teaspoon olive oil
- 2 cloves garlic, minced
- ¼ teaspoon cumin
- salt and pepper

Instructions

1. Place a pan over medium heat. Add olive oil.
2. Add garlic, onion, jalapeno, zucchini, corn to the pan and cook for 6 minutes.
3. Season with cumin, salt and pepper. Set aside.
4. Return skillet to the medium heat, add oil.
5. Add wheat tortilla, onion-garlic mixture, top with vegetable shreds and cook tortilla for 3 minutes on each side until golden brown.
6. Remove from pan, cut into 4 pieces and serve with salsa and guacamole.

Chickpea Avocado Salad Sandwich With Cranberries

Cooking Time: 10 minutes

Servings: 2

Ingredients

- 15 oz. can chickpeas, rinsed and drained
- ¼ cup dried cranberries
- 1 large ripe avocado
- 4 slices gluten free bread, toasted
- 2 teaspoons freshly squeezed lemon juice
- salt and pepper

Instructions

1. Combine chickpeas and avocado in a bowl, Mash until chunky in consistency.
2. Add lemon juice, cranberries, salt and pepper.
3. Spread the mixture on the toasted bread.

Rice Paper Rolls with Mango and Mint

Cooking Time: 20 minutes

Servings: 6

Ingredients

For the rice paper rolls:

- 6 sheets Vietnamese rice paper
- 1 cup fresh mint

- 3 cups lettuce, thinly sliced
- 1 ½ cups glass noodles, cooked
- 1 cup purple cabbage, thinly sliced
- 1 avocado, thinly sliced
- 1 cucumber, chopped
- 3 carrots, thinly sliced
- 1 mango, thinly sliced
- 3 green onions, cut into rings
- 6 radishes, thinly sliced

For the fried sesame tofu:

- 7 oz. block firm tofu, thinly sliced
- 1 teaspoon sesame oil
- 1 tablespoon soy sauce
- 1 tablespoon sesame seeds

For the peanut dipping sauce:

- ¼ cup chunky peanut butter
- 2 teaspoons soy sauce
- 1 clove of garlic, minced
- 4 tablespoons warm water
- ½ teaspoons Sriracha sauce

Instructions

1. Add tap water to a large shallow bowl, dip rice papers, but not for too long.
2. Place a large skillet over medium heat, add sesame oil.
3. Add tofu, soy sauce to the pan and cook for about 5 minutes until browned.
4. Add sesame seeds and cook for 60 seconds.
5. Mix the peanut dipping sauce ingredients in a bowl and set aside.
6. Fill rice papers with vegetables and tofu. Wrap them like a burrito.
7. Serve rolls with a side of peanut dipping sauce.

Turmeric Chickpea Salad Sandwich

Cooking Time: 5 minutes

Servings: 1

Ingredients

- 1 can chickpeas, drained
- 1/3 cup aquafaba (liquid from the chickpea can)
- ½ teaspoon turmeric
- ½ teaspoon onion powder
- 1 clove garlic, minced
- salt and black pepper

Instructions

1. Put all ingredients into a food processor and pulse until the consistency is chunky and not smooth.
2. Put in a bowl and serve.

Mexican Quinoa

Cooking Time: 25 minutes

Servings: 4

Ingredients

- 1 cup quinoa, uncooked and rinsed
- 1 ½ cup vegetable broth
- 3 cups canned diced tomatoes
- 15 oz. can black beans, drained and rinsed
- 2 cups frozen corn

- 1 cup fresh parsley, chopped
- 1 onion, chopped
- 3 cloves of garlic, minced
- 2 bell peppers, chopped
- 1 tablespoon paprika powder
- ½ tablespoon cumin
- 2 tablespoons olive oil
- 2 tablespoons lime juice
- 2 green onions, chopped
- salt and pepper

Instructions

1. Place a large pot over medium heat. Add olive oil.
2. Cook onions for 3 minutes.
3. Add garlic, bell peppers and cook for 5 minutes.
4. Add the remaining ingredients except lime juice, green onions and parsley. Cover and cook for about 20 minutes, keep checking to make sure the quinoa doesn't stick and burn.
5. Add lime juice, green onions and parsley.
6. Season the dish with salt and pepper before serving.

Potato Fritters

Cooking Time: 25 minutes

Servings: 12

Ingredients

For the vegetable potato fritters:

- ¾ cup red lentils, cooked
- 1 onion, chopped
- 2 cloves garlic, minced
- 2 potatoes, grated
- 1 carrot, grated
- 5 tablespoons all-purpose flour

- ½ teaspoon smoked paprika powder
- 1 teaspoon paprika powder
- 1 teaspoon majoram
- salt and black pepper

For the Sriracha mayonnaise:

- 3 tablespoons vegan mayonnaise
- 1 teaspoon tomato paste
- 1 teaspoon garlic powder
- ½ teaspoon smoked paprika powder
- Sriracha sauce
- salt and pepper

Instructions

1. Add red lentils, carrot, potatoes, garlic, onion, flour, smoked paprika, regular paprika, Marjoram, salt and pepper to a large bowl.
2. Place a skillet over medium heat. Heat oil.
3. Scoop 2 tablespoons for each fritter and fry in the pan for about 4 minutes.
4. In a separate bowl combine Sriracha mayonnaise ingredients and set aside.

5. Serve fritters with salad and vegan sriracha mayonnaise.

Tempeh Reuben

Cooking Time: 40 minutes

Servings: 2

Ingredients

For the marinated Tempeh:

- 8 oz. package tempeh, thinly sliced in four
- 1/2 cup vegetable broth
- 1 tablespoon balsamic vinegar
- 1 tablespoon vegan Worcestershire sauce
- 1 teaspoon liquid smoke
- 1 teaspoon onion powder
- 1 teaspoon smoked paprika
- 1/2 teaspoon garlic powder

The remaining ingredients:

- 4 slices Alvarado's Sprouted Rye Seed Bread
- 1/2 heaping cup sauerkraut
- 1/4 cup vegan Russian Dressing
- vegan Swiss cheese, sliced
- 2 tablespoons oil
- 1 tablespoon vegan butter

Instructions

1. Combine broth, balsamic vinegar, Worcestershire sauce, liquid smoke, onion powder, smoked paprika and garlic powder.

2. Add sliced tempeh to the marinade and set aside to marinate for 30 minutes.

3. Place a large skillet over medium heat, add oil.

4. Add marinated tempeh slices and cook for 5 minutes on each side, then add marinade and cook for 3 minutes.

5. Spread butter on the sprouted rye seed bread, place slices on the skillet and cook for 3 minutes on one side. Flip and add the Russian dressing.

6. Divide sauerkraut between two slices, add 2 slices of tempeh, and a slice of vegan Swiss cheese.

7. Add second slice of bread and toast for 5 minutes in the skillet until browned.

8. Remove from skillet and serve.

Broccoli Pesto with Pasta and Cherry Tomatoes

Cooking Time: 5 minutes

Servings: 2

Ingredients

For the broccoli pesto:

- 2 heaped cups broccoli florets, cooked
- ½ cup walnuts
- 3 tablespoons nutritional yeast
- 2 cloves of garlic

- 3 tablespoons olive oil
- 1/2 cup roughly chopped parsley
- salt and black pepper

For the pasta:

- 9 oz. whole wheat pasta, cooked
- 1 cup cherry tomatoes, halved
- 1 cup cooked broccoli florets

Instructions

1. Combine pesto ingredients in a large bowl.
2. Serve cooked pasta with cherry tomatoes, cooked broccoli and pesto.

Korean Barbecue Tempeh Wraps

Cooking Time: 25 minutes

Servings: 4

Ingredients

For the Korean barbecue sauce:

- ¾ cup water
- 1/3 cup soy sauce
- ¼ cup maple syrup
- ¼ cup tomato paste
- 2 tablespoons gochujang
- 2 garlic cloves, minced
- 2 teaspoons ginger, grated
- 1 teaspoon sesame oil

For the Tempeh filling:

- 2 tablespoons vegetable oil
- 2-8 oz. packages tempeh, cubed
- 1 red bell pepper, thinly sliced
- 1 onion, thinly sliced
- 2 scallions, chopped
- 2 teaspoons sesame seeds

For the wraps:

- 4 large flour tortillas
- 4 large lettuce leaves
- 1 large avocado sliced

Instructions

1. Combine the Korean sauce ingredients in a bowl.
2. Place a large skillet over medium heat, add sauce and bring it to a simmer, lower the heat and let it simmer for 10 minutes.
3. Place another skillet over medium heat and add oil.
4. Add and cook tempeh for about 5 minutes.
5. Increase the heat, add bell pepper, onion and cook for 2 minutes, then lower the heat, add sauce and cook for 3 minutes. Once done, remove the from heat and set aside.
6. Put tortilla on a working surface, place lettuce leaves, avocado slices, and tempeh mixture on top. Wrap like a burrito to enclose the fillings inside
7. Do this for all tortillas before serving.

Crab Cakes

Cooking Time: 20 minutes

Servings: 8

Ingredients

- 2 cups cooked chickpeas
- 2 cans artichoke hearts in brine, drained and chopped
- ½ cup onion, chopped
- ¼ cup parsley, chopped
- 2 cloves garlic, minced
- 3 teaspoons fresh lemon juice
- 1 stalk celery, chopped
- 2 teaspoons Dijon mustard
- 3 tablespoons dill, chopped
- 1 cup panko bread crumbs
- 2 teaspoons vegan Worcestershire sauce
- 2 teaspoons fish seasoning
- vegetable oil
- salt and black pepper

Instructions

1. Place a skillet over medium heat. Add oil.
2. Sauté onions for about 2 minutes in the skillet.
3. Add garlic and cook 60 seconds. Remove from the heat and set aside.
4. Place cooked chickpeas in a bowl and mash them with a fork.
5. Add cooked onions, garlic and mix well.
6. Add the rest of the ingredients.

7. Season with salt and peppers. Form eight vegan crab cakes.
8. Place a skillet over medium heat add vegetable oil.
9. Add crab cakes and cook on each side for 3 minutes.

Smoky Black Beans Parsley Chimichurri

Cooking Time: 28 minutes

Servings: 3

Ingredients

For the smoky black beans:

- 2 teaspoons oil
- 15 oz. black beans
- ¼ cup onion, chopped
- ¼ cup bell pepper, chopped
- 2 cloves garlic, minced
- ½ teaspoon cumin powder
- ½ teaspoon chipotle chili pepper powder
- ½ teaspoon smoked paprika
- 1 medium tomato, chopped
- ½ zucchini, chopped

Other fillings:

- Chimichurri
- tortillas
- 2 cups baby spinach
- 2 red bell pepper, thinly sliced

Instructions

1. Place a large skillet over medium heat. Add oil.
2. Add and cook onions, garlic and bell peppers for about 8 minutes.

3. Add cumin, chili, smoked paprika, black beans, zucchini, tomato and salt. Mix, cover and cook on low medium for 10 minutes.
4. Place a large pan over medium heat and warm tortilla and spread Chimichurri on the tortilla.
5. Add black beans on the tortilla, cheese and sprinkle both bell peppers and spinach.
6. Wrap the tortilla before serving.

Tuna Sandwich With Chickpeas

Cooking Time: 10 minutes

Servings: 2

Ingredients

For the vegan tuna salad:

- 1 can chickpeas
- 1 tablespoon dried Wakame seaweed
- 2 tablespoons vegan mayonnaise
- 1 teaspoon soy sauce
- 1 teaspoon lemon juice
- 2 teaspoons dill
- 2 stalks of celery, chopped
- salt and pepper

For the sandwich:

- 4 slices of whole wheat bread
- 1 tomato, thinly sliced
- ¼ cucumber, thinly sliced
- lettuce
- ½ onion, cut into rings

Instructions

1. Crumble the weed and place in a shallow bowl.
2. Add water and let the weed soak for 5 minutes. Drain excess water
3. Place chickpeas in a large bowl and mash it with a fork.
4. To the bowl, add celery, mayonnaise, dill, seaweed, lemon juice, soy sauce, salt and pepper and mix well.

Sweet Potato Toast

Cooking Time: 10 minutes

Servings: 1

Ingredients

- 1 medium sweet potato, washed and sliced to fit into the toaster

For the chickpea topping:

- 1 avocado
- 2 cups can chickpeas, drained and rinsed
- ½ teaspoon sumac
- 1 tablespoon lemon juice
- ½ cup small baby watercress

For the cashew cream pepper topping:

- 1/3 cup cashew cream
- 1 pepper, thinly sliced
- 1 handful baby basil leaves
- cracked pepper to taste
- olive oil to drizzle

Instructions

1. Place sweet potato slices in a toaster and toast on high. Then remove from the toaster and poke. Return slices to the toaster and toast again.
2. Combine avocado, sumac, chickpeas, salt and lemon juice in a bowl. Mash it all together.
3. When sweet potatoes are well toasted, transfer them to a plate.
4. Spoon the chickpea mixture and spread it on sweet potato slices.
5. Sprinkle baby watercress and smear cashew cream on top.
6. Follow with basil leaves, olive oil and cracked pepper.

Chickpeas with Dates, Turmeric, Cinnamon and Almonds

Cooking Time: 2 hours

Servings: 4

Ingredients

- 1 2/3 cups plum tomatoes
- 3 1/2 oz. dates, pitted and halved
- 3 1/3 cups chickpeas, rinsed and drained
- 1.4 oz. flaked almonds, toasted
- 2 tablespoons olive oil
- 4 cloves garlic, chopped
- 1 tablespoon ginger, grated

- 1 handful coriander, stalks and leaves separated and chopped
- 1 teaspoon ground cumin
- 1 teaspoon ground coriander
- 1 teaspoon ground turmeric
- 1 cinnamon stick
- 1 tablespoon lemon juice
- 1 teaspoon lime zest
- 1 orange, cut into wedges
- couscous to serve

Instructions

1. Preheat the slow cooker on low heat.
2. Combine 1 cup tomatoes and half of dates in a blender and blend for about 1 minute.
3. Add this mixture to the slow cooker with the remaining tomatoes.
4. To the slow cooker add oil, garlic, ginger, coriander stalks, spices, lemon zest and 1 cup water. Cook for 6 hours on low until sauce is thick.
5. Add chickpeas and the remaining dates and cook for ½ an hour.
6. Lastly add lemon juice. Remove from the slow cooker.

Cucumber Avocado Toast

Cooking time: 5 minutes

Servings: 2

Ingredients

- 1 cucumber, sliced
- 2 bread slices, toasted
- ¼ handful basil leaves, chopped
- 4 tablespoons avocado, mashed
- Salt and pepper, to taste
- 1 teaspoon lemon juice

Instructions

1-Combine lemon juice together with the mashed avocado, and then spread the mixture on two bread slices.

2 -Top with cucumber slices along with the finely chopped basil leaves.

3-Generously sprinkle with salt and pepper and enjoy!

Tofu Fish Sticks

Cooking time: 45 minutes

Servings: 4

Ingredients

- 1 cup bread crumbs
- 2 tablespoons nori seaweed, crumbled
- 2 blocks tofu, pressed
- 2 tablespoons soy sauce
- 1 teaspoon lemon pepper
- 1/4 cup soy milk
- 2 tablespoons lemon juice

Instructions

1. Preheat the oven to 375F and then cut the tofu into strips. Evenly coat the tofu strips with flour.
2. Whisk the soy milk together with soy sauce and lemon juice in a bowl, and then mix the lemon pepper, breadcrumbs and nori in a separate bowl.
3. When done, dip the tofu in the soy milk mixture and then coat the dipped tofu in the breadcrumb's mixture.
4. Bake for 40-45 minutes flipping only once, until crispy and brown. Alternatively, you can fry the both sides in the pan with little oil.
5. When baked through, serve and enjoy!

Cornmeal Breaded Tofu

Cooking time: 15 minutes

Servings: 4

Ingredients

- 1/4 cup cornmeal
- 1/4 teaspoon cayenne pepper
- 1 block tofu, pressed
- 1 teaspoon chili powder
- 2 tablespoons nutritional yeast
- Salt and pepper, to taste
- 1/4 cup flour
- Olive oil

Instructions

1. Preheat the oven to 400F and use a kitchen brush to lightly coat the baking sheet with oil.
2. Cut the pressed tofu into thin rectangular strips. Mix flour, nutritionist yeast, spices and cornmeal in a bowl until well combined.
3. Add the tofu pieces bit by bit into the cornmeal mixture to coat evenly, and then place the coated tofu pieces on a prepared baking sheet.
4. Bake for 5-7 minutes until lightly browned on one side. Flip the tofu and bake for 5 more minutes until baked through. Serve.

Cooking time: 30 minutes
Servings: 6

Ingredients

- 1 tablespoon olive oil
- 3 large sweet potatoes, washed, peeled, chopped
- 1/4 teaspoon paprika
- cooking spray
- 1 teaspoon cumin
- ½ teaspoon cayenne pepper
- 1/2 teaspoon salt

Instructions

1. Preheat the oven to 400F and prepare the sweet potatoes by washing and peeling them, and then chop the potatoes into wedges lengthwise.

2. Put the sweet potatoes wedges into a bowl and then generously drizzle them with oil and toss well until combined.

3. In a bowl, combine the paprika with salt and cumin, and then mix the ingredients together.

4. Sprinkle the cumin-paprika mixture on the sweet potato wedges and then toss well to combine, until the potatoes wedges are nicely coated with spices and olive oil.

5. Spray the baking sheet with cooking spray and then spread the coated sweet potatoes wedges in one layer on the sheet.

6. Bake the potatoes in the oven for 30 minutes.

7. When baked through, serve the sweet potatoes fries with your desired sauce and enjoy!

Cooking time: 15 minutes

Servings: 8

Ingredients

- 3 oz. water
- 2 1/2 oz. sugar
- 1/2 teaspoon ground turmeric
- 1 oz. coconut oil
- 1/2 teaspoon tartar cream
- 5 oz. flour
- ¾ oz. wheat germ, toasted
- 1 1/2 oz. bread flour
- 1/4 teaspoon baking soda
- 1/4 oz. barley malt syrup
- 1/2 teaspoon salt

Instructions

1. Prepare the crackers. Preheat the oven to 350F and prepare two parchment sheets. Add the sugar, wheat germ, flour, turmeric, tartar cream, coconut oil, bread flour and baking soda to a food processor bowl and blend until combined.

2. Add the barley malt syrup to a glass bowl along with water to dissolve the syrup, and then add into the dry blended mixture and continue processing until stiff dough is formed.

3. Knead the dough lightly on the surface, and then separate the dough into two equal parts.

4. Put the cut parchment sheets on a working surface and sprinkle with flour, and then place one of the dough halves in the middle of the paper. Sprinkle the dough with flour and roll out into the rectangle.

5. Use a pizza cutter cut the dough into bite-size squares and then place the crackers on a sheet pan.

6. Sprinkle the crackers with salt and bake for about 12 minutes. Rotate the pan halfway.

7. Let the crackers cool to a room temperature. When done, serve and enjoy!

Spinach and Artichoke Dip

Cooking time: 40 minutes

Servings: 6-8

Ingredients

- 2 tablespoons nutritional yeast
- 2 tablespoons olive oil
- 1 tablespoon Dijon mustard
- 1 lb. cauliflower, cored, chopped into florets
- 1 tablespoon lemon juice
- 1/4 cup vegan mayonnaise
- 10 oz. spinach
- 14 oz. artichokes drained, halved
- 2 oz. raw cashews
- 2 teaspoons garlic powder
- 1 cup vegetable stock or vegetable broth
- 2 garlic cloves, minced
- Salt and pepper, to taste
- Tortilla chips or pita chips, to serve

Instructions

1. Preheat the oven to 350F and add the vegetable stock to a skillet. Bring the vegetable stock to a simmer over medium heat and then add the cauliflower florets along with cashews and stir well until evenly coated. Set the heat to low and then close the lid. Cook for about 10 minutes until cauliflower florets are tender.

2. When done, transfer the cashews, cauliflower and the liquid to a blender and let cool for a minute. Process the mixture until smooth, and then add the nutritional yeast, mayonnaise, lemon juice, mustard and garlic powder, and continue processing until combined.

3. Use a kitchen towel to wipe the skillet and then add oil and heat on medium heat until warmed through. Add garlic and cook for 1-2 minutes until softened and fragrant, stirring frequently, and then add spinach along with salt. Continue cooking until the spinach wilts.

4. Add the cooked spinach to the blender along with the artichokes, and blend until incorporated.

5. Transfer the dip to a baking dish and bake for 30 minutes until the edges are slightly browned. Flip and bake the other side for about 2-3 minutes until nicely browned.

6. When baked through, serve immediately with chips and enjoy!

Coconut Bacon

Cooking time: 15 minutes

Servings: 6

Ingredients

- 1 teaspoon apple cider vinegar
- 2 tablespoons soy sauce or tamari
- 2 cups plain coconut flakes
- 2 tablespoons maple syrup
- Pepper, to taste
- 1/2 teaspoon smoked paprika

Instructions

1. Preheat the oven to 325F and then add the coconut flakes to a mixing bowl.
2. Add all other ingredients to a separate bowl and then add the coconut flakes. Mix the ingredients together until the coconut flakes are evenly coated.
3. Spread the coated coconut flakes in one layer evenly on a baking sheet and bake for about 10 minutes. Stir and flip the coconut flakes, bake for 3-4 more minutes until nicely browned.
4. When baked through, remove from heat and let cool completely. Slice and serve.

Chapter 3: Delicious Main Dish Recipes for Dinner.

Brown Rice Stir Fry with Vegetables

Cooking time: 25 minutes

Servings: 4

Ingredients

- 1 handful fresh parsley, chopped
- 1/2 zucchini, chopped
- 2 tablespoons olive oil
- 2 tablespoons soy sauce
- 1/2 bell pepper, chopped
- 1/2 cup brown rice, uncooked
- 4 garlic cloves, minced
- 1 cup red cabbage, chopped
- 1/8 teaspoon cayenne powder
- 1/2 broccoli head, chopped
- Sesame seeds, for garnish

Instructions

1. Cook the brown rice as per the package instructions.
2. Bring water to a boil in a frying pan and then add veggies and make sure they are fully covered with water. Cook for 1-2 minutes on high heat, and then drain the water and set aside.
3. Add oil to the wok pan and heat over high heat and then add garlic along with parsley and cayenne powder. Cook for a minute stirring frequently and then add the drained veggies, tamari and the cooked rice.
4. Cook for 1-2 minutes and then garnish with sesame seeds if desired. Serve and enjoy!

Grilled Veggie Skewers

Cooking time: 15 minutes

Servings: 4-6

Ingredients

- 1 red onion, peeled, chopped
- 2 tablespoons avocado oil
- 2 portobello mushrooms, chopped
- 1 sweet potato, chopped
- 2 bell peppers, chopped

- 6 baby red potatoes, quartered
- Salt and black pepper, to taste
- 4 ears corn

Instructions

1. Preheat the oven to 375F and add the sweet potato to a cooking pot along with the quartered potatoes and water. Bring to a boil and cook until lightly tender for about 10 minutes. When done, drain the water and let cool a bit.
2. Thread the vegetables onto skewers, and then brush them evenly with oil. When done, season the vegetables generously with salt and pepper on each side.
3. Cook the vegetables for about 10-15 minutes until tender and cooked through. Flip halfway. Place the corn directly on the vegetables to cook together.
4. When done, serve and enjoy with the desired sauce.

Eggplant Teriyaki Bowls

Cooking time: 45 minutes

Servings: 4

INGREDIENTS

- 1 carrot, shredded
- 1 chucky eggplant
- ¼ cup edamame beans, frozen
- 1 lime, ½ sliced, ½ juiced
- 2 spring onions , chopped

- 1 ½ tablespoons vegetable oil
- 1 handful radishes, sliced
- 1 tablespoon caster sugar
- 1 garlic clove, crushed
- ½ cup jasmine rice
- 2 tablespoons sesame seeds, toasted
- 1 small ginger, grated
- 2 tablespoons soy sauce

INSTRUCTIONS

1. Add 2 cups of water to a cooking pan, add rice and salt to taste. Bring to a boil, cook for a minute, and then close the lid. Reduce the heat to low and cook for 10 minutes until cooked through. Turn off the heat and steam for additional 10 minutes.

2. Add a tablespoon of oil to a bowl and toss the eggplant in it. Preheat the wok pan, add the eggplant and cook for 5 minutes, stirring often, until lightly softened and charred. Add the carrots to the wok along with garlic, ginger and spring onions, and then fry for 2-3 minutes.

3. In a small bowl, whisk the sugar along with soy sauce and a cup of water and then add into the wok. Simmer until the eggplant is very soft, for about 10-15 minutes.

4. Add water to the pan and bring to a boil and then add the frozen edamame beans, remove the beans, drain and rinse them well under running water. Add the radishes to a bowl, drain the beans again and then add them to the radishes. Squeeze lime juice on top and toss well until combined.

5. Serve the rice in the bowls and then scoop the eggplant and sauce on top along with the beans and radishes. Sprinkle with sesame seeds and garnish with the lime slices. Enjoy

Cooking time: 45 minutes

Servings: 8

Ingredients

- 3 cups vegetable stock
- 1 onion, chopped
- 1 cup quinoa, rinsed, drained
- 1 red chilli, chopped
- 2 teaspoons ground cumin
- 1 lb. tomatoes, chopped
- olive oil spray
- 1 teaspoon smoked paprika
- 1 small avocado, sliced
- ½ teaspoon chilli powder
- 2 garlic cloves, crushed
- 1 lb. black beans, rinsed, drained
- Coriander leaves, to serve

Instructions

1. Generously grease the cooking pan with oil and place over medium heat and then add the onion, red chili and garlic. Fry the ingredients until soft, and then add spices and stir.

2. Add the vegetable stock into the pan along with quinoa, black beans and tomatoes, and then adjust the seasonings if needed.

3. Close the lid and simmer until quinoa is tender, for about 30 minutes.

4. When done, garnish with coriander leaves and top with the avocado slices. Serve and enjoy!

Cooking Time: 20 minutes

Servings: 4

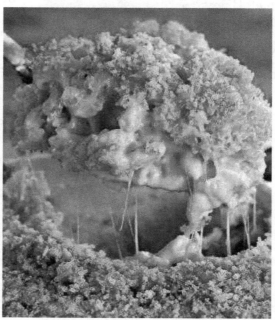

Ingredients

- 8 oz. whole-grain macaroni elbows, cooked
- 1 head of broccoli, florets
- 1 ½ tablespoons avocado oil
- 1 onion, chopped
- 1 cup potato, peeled and grated
- 3 cloves garlic, minced
- ½ teaspoon garlic powder
- ½ teaspoon onion powder
- ½ teaspoon dry mustard powder

- 1 small pinch red pepper flakes
- ⅔ cup raw cashews
- 1 cup water, or more if needed
- ¼ cup nutritional yeast
- 3 teaspoons apple cider vinegar
- salt

Instructions

1. Place a large pot over medium heat. Add salt and water and bring to a boil.
2. Add broccoli and cook for 5 minutes. Once done, drain excess liquid and set aside in a large mixing bowl.
3. Place a large skillet over medium heat. Add oil.
4. Add onion, salt and cook for about 5 minutes.
5. Add potatoes, garlic, garlic powder, onion powder, mustard powder, salt, red pepper flakes and cook for 60 seconds.
6. Add cashews, water, bring mixture to a simmer, reduce the heat and let it cook until potatoes are tender. Remove from the heat.
7. Pour the mixture into a food processor, add nutritional yeast, vinegar and pulse until the mixture is smooth, adding water if necessary.
8. Serve cooked pasta in bowls, topped with the blended mixture.

Butternut Squash Linguine With Fried Sage

Cooking Time: 25 minutes

Servings: 4

Ingredients

- 3 cups butternut squash, peeled, seeded, and chopped
- 2 cups vegetable broth
- 12 oz. whole grain fettucine, cooked, 1 cup cooking liquid saved
- 1 onion, chopped

- 2 garlic cloves, pressed
- 2 tablespoons olive oil
- 1 tablespoon fresh sage, chopped
- ⅛ teaspoon red pepper flakes
- salt and pepper

Instructions

1. Place a large pan over medium heat. Add oil.
2. Add sage and cook it until crispy. Season with salt and set aside.
3. Return the same pan to medium heat, add butternut, onion, garlic, red pepper flakes, salt and pepper. Cook for about 10 minutes.
4. Add broth and bring to a boil, then reduce the heat and let it cook for 20 minutes.
5. Place a pot of salty water over medium heat.
6. Cool the squash mixture and blend the mixture until smooth with a mixer.
7. Add pasta, ¼ cup reserved pasta liquid to the pan, return pan to medium heat and cook for 3 minutes.

Paella

Cooking Time: 1 hour

Servings: 6

Ingredients

- 15 oz. diced tomatoes, drained
- 2 cups short-grain brown rice
- 1 ½ cups cooked chickpeas
- 3 cups vegetable broth
- ⅓ cup dry white wine
- 1 14 oz. artichokes, drained and chopped
- ½ cup Kalamata olives, pitted and halved
- ¼ cup parsley, chopped
- ½ cup peas
- 3 tablespoons extra-virgin olive oil, divided
- 1 onion, chopped
- 6 garlic cloves, pressed or minced
- 2 teaspoons smoked paprika
- ½ teaspoon saffron threads, crumbled
- 2 bell peppers, stemmed, seeded and sliced
- 2 tablespoons lemon juice
- salt and pepper

Instructions

1. Preheat the oven to 350F.
2. Place a large skillet over medium heat and add 2 tablespoons oil.
3. Add onion, salt and cook for 5 minutes.
4. Add garlic, paprika and cook for ½ a minute.

5. Add tomatoes and stir well. Cook until the mixture starts to thicken.
6. Add rice and cook for 1 minute while stirring.
7. Add chickpeas, broth, wine, saffron and salt to taste. Increase the heat and bring the mixture to a boil. Remove from the heat.
8. Cover and immediately transfer to an oven on lower rack. Bake for 1 hour.
9. Prepare a baking sheet by lining it with parchment paper. Combine artichokes, peppers, olives, 1 tablespoon olive oil, salt and pepper. Mix well and roast vegetables on the upper rack in the oven for 45 minutes.
10. Add parsley and lemon juice to the baking pan and mix well.
11. Sprinkle the roasted vegetables and peas on the baked rice.

Spicy Thai Peanut Sauce Over Roasted Sweet Potatoes and Rice

Cooking Time: 1 hour 30 minutes

Servings: 4

Ingredients

For the spicy Thai peanut sauce:

- ½ cup creamy peanut butter
- ¼ cup reduced-sodium tamari
- 3 tablespoons apple cider vinegar
- 2 tablespoons honey or maple syrup
- 1 teaspoon grated fresh ginger
- 2 cloves garlic, pressed
- ¼ teaspoon red pepper flakes
- 2 tablespoons water

For the roasted vegetables:

- 2 sweet potatoes, peeled and sliced
- 1 bell pepper, cored, deseeded, and sliced
- about 2 tablespoons coconut oil (or olive oil)
- ¼ teaspoon cumin powder
- salt

For the rice and garnishes:

- 1 ¼ cup jasmine brown rice
- 2 green onions, sliced
- a handful of cilantro, torn
- a handful of peanuts, crushed

Instructions

1. Place a pot of water on medium heat and bring it to a boil.

2. Preheat the oven to 425F.

3. On a rimmed baking sheet, mix sweet potato, 1 tablespoon coconut oil, cumin and salt. Roast in the middle rack for about 35 minutes.

4. On another baking sheet, mix bell pepper with 1 teaspoon coconut oil, salt and mix well, Roast on the top rack for about 20 minutes until tender.

5. When water is boiling in the pot add rice and mix well. Cook for about 30 minutes and drain excess liquid. Once done, cover and let it sit for 10 minutes, fluff it after.

6. Mix sauce ingredients in a small bowl and set aside.

7. Divide rice, roasted vegetables in bowls and top with sauce, green onions, cilantro and peanuts before serving.

Butternut Squash Chipotle Chili With Avocado

Cooking Time: 20 minutes

Servings: 4

Ingredients

- 3 cups black beans, cooked
- 14 oz. can diced tomatoes, including the liquid
- 2 cups vegetable broth
- 1 onion, chopped
- 2 bell peppers, chopped
- 1 small butternut squash, cubed
- 4 garlic cloves, minced
- 2 tablespoons olive oil
- 1 tablespoon chili powder
- ½ tablespoon chopped chipotle pepper in adobo
- 1 teaspoon ground cumin
- ¼ teaspoon ground cinnamon
- 1 bay leaf
- 2 avocados, diced
- 3 corn tortillas for crispy tortilla strips
- salt

Instructions

1. Place a stockpot over medium heat. Add oil.
2. Add and cook onion, bell peppers and butternut squash for about 5 minutes.
3. Reduce the heat, add garlic, chili powder, ½ tablespoon chopped chipotle peppers, cumin and cinnamon. Cook for ½ a minute.

4. Add bay leaves, black beans, tomatoes and their juices and broth. Mix well. Cook for about 1 hour. Remove bay leaf when done cooking.

5. Slice corn tortillas into thin little strips.

6. Place a pan over medium heat and add olive oil. Add tortilla strips and season with salt. Cook until crispy for about 7 minutes. Remove from the heat and place in a bowl covered with paper towel to drain excess oil.

7. Serve chili in bowls, topped with crispy tortilla chips and avocado.

Chickpea Biryani

Cooking Time: 40 minutes

Servings: 6

Ingredients

- 4 cups veggie stock
- 2 cups basmati rice, rinsed
- 1 can chickpeas, drained, rinsed
- ½ cup raisins
- 1 large onion, thinly sliced
- 2 cups thinly sliced veggies (bell pepper, zucchini and carrots)
- 3 garlic cloves, chopped
- 1 tablespoon ginger, chopped
- 1 tablespoon cumin
- 1 tablespoon coriander
- 1 teaspoon chili powder
- 1 teaspoon cinnamon
- ½ teaspoon cardamom
- ½ teaspoon turmeric
- 2 tablespoons olive oil
- 1 bay leaf
- salt

Instructions

1. Place a large skillet over medium high heat. Add oil.
2. Sauté onions for about 5 minutes.
3. Reduce the heat to medium, add vegetables, garlic and ginger. Cook for 5 minutes. Scoop 1 cup of this mixture and set aside.
4. Add spices, bay leaf and rice. Stir for about 1 minute.
5. Add stock and salt to taste.

6. Add chickpeas, raisins and 1 cup of vegetables. Bring the mixture to a simmer over high heat.

7. Lower the heat, cover tightly and let it simmer for ½ an hour. Remove from the heat when rice is done.

Chinese Eggplant

Cooking Time: 45 minutes

Servings: 4

Ingredients

- 1 ½ lbs. eggplants, chopped
- 2 cups water
- 2 tablespoons cornstarch

- 4 tablespoons peanut oil
- 4 cloves garlic, chopped
- 2 teaspoons ginger, minced
- 10 dried red chilies
- salt

For the Szechuan sauce:

- 1 teaspoon Szechuan peppercorns
- ¼ cup soy sauce
- 1 tablespoon garlic chili paste
- 1 tablespoon sesame oil
- 1 tablespoon rice vinegar
- 1 tablespoon Chinese cooking wine
- 3 tablespoons coconut sugar
- ½ teaspoon five spice

Instructions

1. Place chopped eggplants in a shallow bowl. Add water and 2 teaspoons salt. Stir cover and let it sit for about 15 minutes.
2. Meanwhile place a small pan over medium heat. Toast the Szechuan peppercorns for about 2 minutes and crush them.

3. Add crushed peppercorns to a medium bowl, add soy, chili paste, sesame oil, rice vinegar, Chinese cooking vinegar, coconut sugar and five spice.
4. Drain excess liquid from the eggplants and toss in the corn starch.
5. Place a large skillet over medium heat, add eggplants and cook them until golden. Set aside.
6. Add 1 tablespoon of oil in the skillet placed over medium heat. Cook garlic and ginger for 2 minutes.
7. Add dried chilies and cook for 1 minute. Add the Szechuan sauce and bring the mixture to a simmer in 20 seconds.
8. Add back eggplants and cook for about 60 seconds.

Black Pepper Tofu with Bok Choy

Cooking Time: 30 minutes

Servings: 2

Ingredients

- 12 oz. firm tofu, cubed
- 1/3 cup corn starch for dredging
- 2 tablespoons coconut oil
- 1 teaspoon fresh cracked peppercorns

- 1 shallot, sliced
- 4 cloves garlic, chopped
- 6 oz. baby bok choy, sliced to 4 slices

For the black pepper sauce:

- 2 tablespoons soy sauce
- 2 tablespoons Chinese cooking wine
- 2 tablespoons water
- 1 teaspoon brown sugar
- ½ teaspoon fresh cracked peppercorns
- 1 teaspoon chili paste

Instructions

1. In a small bowl, combine wok sauce ingredients and mix well until sugar dissolves. Set aside.
2. Place cornstarch in a shallow bowl and dredge tofu in the cornstarch. Set aside.
3. Place a large skillet over medium heat. Heat 1 tablespoon coconut oil.
4. Add peppercorns and toast for about 1 minute.
5. Add tofu and cook on all sides for about 6 minutes. Set tofu aside.
6. Add the remaining coconut oil. Add shallots, garlic and bok choy. Cook for 8 minutes.
7. Add back the tofu and cook for less than a minute.

Spaghetti Alla Puttanesca

Cooking Time: 30 minutes

Servings: 4

Ingredients

For the Puttanesca sauce:

- 28 oz. can chunky tomato sauce

- ⅓ cup chopped Kalamata olives
- ⅓ cup capers
- 1 tablespoon Kalamata olive brine
- 1 tablespoon caper brine
- 3 cloves garlic, minced
- ¼ teaspoon red pepper flakes
- 1 tablespoon olive oil
- ½ cup parsley leaves, chopped and divided
- salt and pepper

For the pasta:

- 8 oz. whole grain spaghetti
- 6 oz. zucchini noodles

Instructions

1. Place a medium skillet over medium heat.
2. Add tomato sauce, olives, capers, olive brine, caper brine, garlic and red pepper flakes. Bring the mixture to a boil, reduce the heat and let it simmer for 20 minutes. Remove from the heat and set aside.
3. Place a pot over medium heat. Add water, salt, spaghetti and cook as directed on package. When done, drain excess water.
4. Pour the sauce over pasta and mix well.
5. Add zucchini noodles before serving.

Thai Red Curry

Cooking Time: 40 minutes

Servings: 4

Ingredients

- 1 ¼ cups brown jasmine rice, rinsed
- 1 tablespoon coconut oil
- 1 cup onion, chopped
- 1 tablespoon fresh ginger, ginger
- 2 cloves garlic, minced

- 1 red bell pepper, sliced
- 1 yellow bell pepper, sliced
- 3 carrots, peeled and sliced
- 2 tablespoons Thai red curry paste
- 1 14 oz. can coconut milk
- ½ cup water
- 1 ½ cups packed kale, chopped
- 1 ½ teaspoons coconut sugar
- 1 tablespoon tamari
- 2 teaspoons fresh lime juice

Instructions

1. Place a large pot over medium heat and add water. Bring it to a boil.
2. Add rice, salt and cook for 30 minutes. Remove from the heat, cover and let it sit for 10 minutes.
3. Place a large pan over medium heat. Add oil.
4. Cook onion and salt for about 5 minutes.
5. Add garlic, ginger and cook for about ½ a minute.
6. Add bell peppers, carrots and cook for about 5 minutes.
7. Add curry paste and cook for additional 2 minutes.
8. Add coconut milk, water, kale, sugar, tamari and lime juice. Remove from the heat.

Thai Green Curry with Spring Vegetables

Cooking Time: 45 minutes

Servings: 4

Ingredients

- 1 cup brown basmati rice, rinsed
- 2 teaspoons coconut oil
- 1 onion, diced
- 1 tablespoon fresh ginger, chopped
- 2 cloves garlic, chopped
- 2 cups asparagus, sliced
- 1 cup carrots, peeled and sliced

- 2 tablespoons Thai green curry paste
- 14 oz. full-fat coconut milk (I used full-fat coconut milk for a richer curry)
- ½ cup water
- 1 ½ teaspoons coconut sugar
- 2 cups packed baby spinach, chopped
- 1 ½ teaspoons fresh lime juice
- 1 ½ teaspoons tamari
- salt

Instructions

1. Place a pot over medium heat. Add water and bring it to a boil.
2. Add rice, salt to taste and cook for 30 minutes. When done, cover the rice and set aside for more than 10 minutes.
3. Place a large skillet over medium heat. Add oil.
4. Cook onion, garlic, ginger and a pinch of salt.
5. Add asparagus, carrots and cook for 3 minutes.
6. Add curry paste and cook for additional 2 minutes.
7. Add coconut milk, ½ cup water, sugar and bring this mixture to a simmer. Reduce the heat and let it cook for 10 minutes until vegetables are tender.
8. Add spinach and let it cook for ½ a minute. Remove from the heat and season with rice vinegar and tamari.

Tamarind Potato Curry

Cooking Time: 1 hour

Servings: 4

Ingredients

- 26.5 oz. potatoes, peeled and cubed
- 1 onion
- 1 garlic clove
- 1-inch ginger, chopped
- 1 green chilli, chopped
- oil for frying
- 1 teaspoon cumin seeds

- ½ teaspoon fennel seeds
- 1 teaspoon ground coriander
- 1 teaspoon chilli powder
- 14 oz. plum tomatoes
- 2 teaspoon brown sugar
- 2 tablespoons tamarind paste
- 1 handful coriander leaves
- rice or naan bread, to serve

Instructions

1. Place a pot of water over medium heat. Add salt and potatoes. Bring to a boil.
2. Place onion, garlic, ginger, chili, and 2 tablespoons water in a food processor. Pulse until smooth.
3. Place a pan over medium heat. Add oil.
4. Toast cumin and fennel seeds until they pop.
5. Add spices, puree and cook for 5 minutes.
6. Add tomatoes, sugar, tamarind and let it simmer for 10 minutes.
7. Add potatoes and some water. Cover and let it cook until tender.
8. Serve with rice or naan bread.

West African Stew with Sweet Potato and Greens

Cooking Time: 1 hour

Servings: 4

Ingredients

- 1/5 cup crunchy peanut butter
- 1/3 cup coconut cream
- 3 cups vegetable stock
- 21 oz. sweet potatoes, cubed
- 2 cups okra, halved
- 1 cup loosely packed kale, chopped
- 2 onions, 1 roughly chopped and 1 diced
- 1-inch ginger, chopped

- 3 garlic cloves
- 1 scotch bonnet chilli
- 4 tablespoons tomato purée
- sunflower oil
- 2 teaspoons coriander seeds, toasted and crushed
- 2 teaspoons ground cumin
- salt

Instructions

1. Combine roughly chopped onion, ginger, garlic, scotch bonnet, tomato puree and peanut butter in a blender. Blend for 1 minute until paste forms.
2. Place a cast iron pan over medium heat. Add 2 tablespoons sunflower oil.
3. Add diced onions and cook for 5 minutes. Season with salt.
4. Add spices, peanut sauce and cook for 5 minutes.
5. Add coconut cream, stock and bring it to a simmer for about 10 minutes.
6. Add cubed sweet potatoes, cover and cook for about 15 minutes.
7. Add okra, kale and cook for 10 additional minutes.
8. Remove from heat before serving.

Kale Slaw

Cooking Time: 15 minutes

Servings: 4

Ingredients

- 1 small bunch kale, chopped
- ½ small head cabbage, shredded
- ¼ onion, thinly sliced
- ¼ cup tender herbs (cilantro, basil, parsley, chives)
- ¼ cup olive oil
- 4 tablespoons lemon juice
- 2 garlic cloves, minced
- salt, pepper and chili flakes

Instructions

1. Combine kale, cabbage, herbs and onions in a large bowl.
2. Add olive oil, lemon juice, minced garlic, salt, pepper and mix well.
3. Add chili flakes, toss well before serving.

Chapter 4: Soups and Salads

Moroccan Veggie Soup

Cooking Time: 45 minutes

Servings: 4

Ingredients

- 1 2/3 cups chopped tomatoes
- 1 2/3 chickpeas, drained and rinsed
- 1 cup loosely spinach, chopped
- 2 teaspoons vegetable oil
- 1 onion, chopped

- 3 celery sticks, chopped
- 3 garlic cloves, chopped
- 2 preserved lemons, flesh discarded and rind finely chopped
- 2 red chili, deseeded and chopped
- 1 tablespoon tomato purée
- 2 teaspoons ground cumin
- 1 teaspoon ground turmeric
- ½ teaspoon ground cinnamon
- 1 potato, chopped
- 1 bunch flat-leaf parsley, chopped
- 4 tablespoons lemon juice

Instructions

1. Place a large pan over medium heat. Add onion celery and salt. Cover and cook for 10 minutes.
2. Add garlic, preserved lemons, red chilies and cook for 2 minutes.
3. Add tomato puree, spices and cook for 2 minutes.
4. Add chopped tomatoes, potato, chickpeas and 5 cups of boiling water. Bring to a boil and let it simmer for 30 minutes.
5. Add spinach, parsley and lemon juice before serving.

Tex Mex Black Bean and Avocado Salad

Cooking Time: 15 minutes

Servings: 2

Ingredients

- 14 oz. black beans, drained and rinsed
- 3 jars roasted red peppers, chopped
- 1 avocado, chopped
- ½ onion, chopped
- 1 red chili, chopped
- 1 lime, plus wedges to serve
- olive oil
- 1 teaspoon cumin seeds
- 2 handfuls rocket
- 2 pitta breads, warmed

Instructions

1. Combine beans, peppers, avocado, onion and chili in a large mixing bowl.
2. Add lime juice, cumin seeds and mix well.
3. Serve the rocket on two plates with warm pittas and divide the bean mixture.

Lentil Fattoush Salad

Cooking Time: 50 minutes

Servings: 2

Ingredients

- ⅓ cup dry green lentils
- 1 whole wheat pita pocket, chopped into bite sized pieces
- 2 teaspoons olive oil
- 2 teaspoons zaatar
- 4 cups loosely packed arugula
- 2 stalks celery, chopped
- 1 carrot stick, chopped
- ¼ small hothouse cucumber, chopped
- 1 small radish, thinly sliced
- ¼ cup dates, chopped
- 2 tablespoons toasted sunflower seeds

For the maple Dijon vinaigrette:

- 2 tablespoons olive oil
- 2 tablespoons balsamic vinegar
- 1 tablespoon Dijon mustard
- 1 tablespoon maple syrup

Instructions

1. Place a small pot over medium heat. Add lentils and 2/3 cup water.
2. Bring it to a boil, lower the heat and bring it to a simmer for 35 minutes. Remove from the heat and drain excess liquid.
3. Preheat the oven to 425F. Line a baking sheet with parchment paper.
4. Mix pita pieces with olive oil and zaatar. Place on a baking sheet and bake for 7 minutes.
5. Mix arugula, lentils, veggies, dates, sunflower seeds and pita croutons.
6. Meanwhile in a separate bowl, mix the dressing ingredients and set aside.
7. Add the dressing and toss well before serving.

Cooking Time: 35 minutes

Servings: 4

Ingredients

- 2 sweet potatoes, peeled and cubed
- 1 tablespoon olive oil
- ½ teaspoon each of paprika, oregano and cayenne pepper
- 1 shallot, diced
- 2 spring onions, chopped
- 1 small bunch chives, chopped
- 3 tablespoons red wine vinegar
- 2 teaspoons olive oil
- 1 tablespoon pure maple syrup
- salt and pepper

Instructions

1. Preheat the oven to 300F and prepare a baking sheet by lining it with parchment paper.
2. Place sweet potatoes in the baking sheet.
3. Drizzle some olive oil and spices, toss well and bake for 30 minutes.

4. In a separate bowl, mix shallots, scallions, chives, vinegar, olive oil and maple syrup.

5. Add baked sweet potatoes to the dressing.

Lentil Salad with Spinach and Pomegranate

Cooking Time: 15 minutes

Servings: 3

Ingredients

For the vegan lentil salad:

- 3 cups brown lentils, cooked
- 1 avocado, cut into slices
- 2-3 handfuls fresh spinach
- ½ cup walnuts, chopped
- 2 apples, chopped
- 1 pomegranate

For the tahini orange dressing:

- 3 tablespoons tahini
- 2 tablespoons olive oil
- 1 clove of garlic
- 6 tablespoons water
- 4 tablespoons orange juice
- 2 teaspoons orange zest
- salt and pepper

Instructions

1. Prepare lentils according to package instructions.
2. Place pomegranate in a shallow bowl filled with water, cut in half and take out seeds, remove fibers floating on the water.
3. Process all dressing ingredients in a food processor. Process until smooth and set aside.

4. Place salad ingredients in a large bowl and mix well.
5. Drizzle dressing over salad before serving.

Broccoli Salad Curry Dressing

Cooking Time: 30 minutes

Servings: 6

Ingredients

- ½ cup plain, unsweetened vegan yogurt
- ¼ cup onion, chopped
- 2 heads broccoli florets, chopped
- 2 stalks celery, chopped
- ½ teaspoon curry powder
- ¼ teaspoon salt or to taste
- 2 tablespoons sunflower seeds

Instructions

1. Mix yoghurt, curry powder and salt.
2. Toss broccoli florets, celery onion and sunflower seeds.
3. Drizzle the dressing on top and put the salad in the fridge for 30 minutes.

Broccoli Cauliflower Soup

Cooking Time: 35 minutes

Servings: 8

Ingredients

- 1 medium head broccoli, finely chopped
- 1 medium head cauliflower, chopped
- ¼ cup whole wheat pastry flour
- 4 cups vegetable broth
- 1 cup unsweetened, unflavored almond milk
- 1/3 cup nutritional yeast

- 2 tablespoons olive oil
- 1 medium onion, chopped
- 2 cloves garlic, minced
- 2 carrots, diced
- 1 potato, diced
- 1 tablespoon lemon juice
- salt and pepper

Instructions

1. Place a skillet over medium heat. Add oil.
2. Add and cook onion, salt, pepper for about 5 minutes.
3. Add garlic and cook for about 1 minute.
4. Add carrots, broccoli, cauliflower, potato and cook for 5 minutes.
5. Add flour and mix.
6. Add broth, almond milk, nutritional yeast and bring the mixture to a boil. Reduce the heat, cover and cook for 20 minutes. Remove from the heat and add lemon juice.
7. Use immersion blender to blend until chunky before serving.

Cooking Time: 50 minutes

Servings: 6

Ingredients

- 1 lb. carrots, peeled and chopped
- 3 cups vegetable broth
- 1 cup vanilla almond milk
- 1 apple, diced
- 1 onion, diced
- 3 tablespoons avocado oil
- 1 teaspoon garlic, minced
- 1 tablespoon ginger, minced
- ½ teaspoon turmeric

Instructions

1. Preheat the oven to 425F and line a baking sheet with parchment paper.
2. Place carrots on the baking sheet and drizzle olive oil, salt and pepper. Bake for 30 minutes and set aside to cool.
3. Combine broth, milk, garlic, ginger, turmeric and vegetables in a food processor. Season with salt and pepper. Pulse until smooth and creamy.
4. Warm the creamy mixture with carrots on a stove before serving.

Persimmon Butternut Squash Soup

Cooking Time: 1 hour

Servings: 4

Ingredients

- 2 cups butternut squash, peeled and chopped
- 3 tablespoons olive oil
- 1 tablespoon butter
- ½ cup onion, chopped
- 3 persimmons, peeled and diced

- 18 oz. vegetable broth
- 1 cup coconut milk
- 1/8 teaspoon ground cloves
- ¼ teaspoon cinnamon
- ½ teaspoon paprika
- ¼ teaspoon ground ginger
- 1 tablespoon maple syrup
- salt and pepper

Instructions

1. Preheat the oven to 400F, Line a baking sheet with parchment paper.
2. Place squash on the baking sheet and season with oil, cinnamon and salt. Bake for 25 minutes.
3. Meanwhile place a pot over medium heat.
4. Add butter and cook onions for 2 minutes.
5. Add squash, persimmon and cook for 5 minutes.
6. Add broth, milk, spices, maple syrup and bring it to a boil. Cover, reduce the heat and let it simmer for 20 minutes.
7. Remove from the heat and blend with an immersion blender until creamy and smooth.
8. Return to medium heat, add the remaining spices, salt and pepper before serving.

Eggplant Tomato Soup

Cooking Time: 35 minutes

Servings: 4

Ingredients

- ½ cup raw cashews
- 1 eggplant, cubed
- 5 large tomatoes, cored and diced
- 1 onion, chopped
- 3 garlic cloves
- ¼ cup extra virgin olive oil
- 1 ½ cup vegetable broth
- 1 tablespoon tamari
- 1 tablespoon fresh oregano

- 1 tablespoon fresh basil
- salt and pepper

Instructions

1. Preheat the oven to 400F and line a large baking sheet with foil.
2. Place a small pan over medium heat, add 2 cups water and bring it to a boil. Remove from the heat, add cashews and set aside to soak for 30 minutes.
3. Place eggplants, tomatoes, onion, garlic and a drizzle of olive oil, salt and pepper. Bake for 20 minutes until tender.
4. Place baked vegetables, soaked cashews, vegetable broth, tamari herbs and pulse for 1 minute until smooth.
5. Return to the skillet and heat the soup again before serving.

Black Bean Soup

Cooking Time: 35 minutes

Servings: 4

Ingredients

- 3 15 oz. cans organic black beans
- 1 15 oz. can organic tomato sauce
- ¾ cup vegetable broth
- 1 teaspoon olive oil

- 1 white onion, chopped
- 3 cloves garlic, minced
- 1 ½ tablespoons chili powder
- 2 teaspoons cumin
- 1 teaspoon dried oregano
- 1/8 teaspoon cayenne pepper
- salt

Instructions

1. Place a pot over medium heat, add oil.
2. Add and cook onions, garlic and cook for 5 minutes.
3. Add in chili powder, cumin, oregano, cayenne pepper and black pepper.
4. Add black beans, tomato sauce, broth and cook for 30 seconds. Bring to a boil, reduce the heat and let it simmer for 25 minutes.

Chapter 5: Desserts and Snacks

Vegan Chocolate

Cooking time: 15 minutes + freezing

Servings: 7

Ingredients

- 1/2 cup cocoa powder, unsweetened
- 1 cup cocoa butter, chopped
- 1 teaspoon vanilla extract
- 5 tablespoons maple syrup
- Salt, to taste

Instructions

1. On a baking sheet, arrange 14 mini cup liners and set aside.
2. Add 2 inches of water to a saucepan and place over medium heat and bring to a boil, and then place a mixing bowl on the top of the pan ensuring it does not touch the water. Add cocoa butter to the mixing bowl and stir well for 2-3 minutes until melted, and then add maple syrup and stir thoroughly with a wooden spoon until well combined. When done, turn off the heat, set the saucepan aside and place the mixing bowl on a flat surface.
3. Add cocoa or cacao powder to the mixing bowl along with vanilla and salt. Whisk the ingredients until well combined and no clumps are left. When done, adjust salt to taste.
4. Carefully pour the prepared chocolate into the mini cupcake liners and season with additional salt.
5. Place the chocolate in the refrigerator or freezer for at least 10 minutes, and then serve. Enjoy!

Peanut Butter Cup Cookies

Cooking time: 25 minutes

Servings: 6-8

Ingredients

- 1/4 cup creamy peanut butter, salted
- 1/2 cup vegan butter, softened
- 3/4 teaspoon baking powder
- 2/3 cup almond flour
- Salt, to taste
- 1 teaspoon vanilla extract
- 3 tablespoons chickpea brine
- 2/3 cup organic cane sugar
- 1 1/3 cups flour blend
- 1/4 cup cornstarch, or arrowroot
- 18 mini vegan peanut butter cups

Instructions

1. Preheat the oven to 375F and prepare two baking sheets by lining them with parchment paper, and then set aside.

2. Place the vegan butter into a mixing bowl and beat for about a minute until the creamy and smooth. Add sugar to the mixing bowl and process for another minute until light and fluffy, and then add chickpea brine along with vanilla and mix once again.

3. When done, add the peanut butter, mix again and then add the baking powder along with salt. Blend the mixture well until combined. Finally add the cornstarch into the mixing bowl along with almond flour and flour blend, and then process on low speed until all the ingredients are well combined.

4. When done, make sure the dough is thick. Place the dough into the refrigerator and chill for at least 15 minutes.

5. Measure 1 ½ tablespoons of the dough and gently roll into balls. Evenly arrange the balls on the lined baking sheets, and smash the balls slightly by pressing them down with the hand.

6. Bake for 10-12 minutes, then top each cookie with the peanut butter cups and press them down lightly.

7. Let cool slightly and serve.

Cooking time: 20 minutes + chilling

Servings: 4

Ingredients

For the crust:

- ¾ cup cashews
- 1 cup coconut, shredded
- 2 tablespoons coconut oil, melted
- 2 tablespoons lemon juice
- 2 tablespoons maple syrup
- 1 teaspoon lemon zest

For the filling:

- ¼ cup maple syrup
- ¼ cup coconut milk
- 1 cup cashews, soaked for 4 hours in cold water
- ⅓ cup coconut oil

- 1 teaspoon vanilla extract
- ¼ teaspoon salt
- 1 tablespoon lemon zest
- ½ cup lemon juice

Instructions

1. Grease the cooking pan lightly with coconut oil.
2. Prepare the crust. Add coconut and cashews to a blender and process until combined and the cashews are broken into small pieces. Then add the coconut oil along with lemon juice, maple syrup and the lemon zest and process again until combined.
3. Press the crust evenly into the prepared pan, to the bottom and sides, and then set aside.
4. Add all the filling ingredients into the blender and process until the mixture is silky and creamy, for about 2-4 minutes. When done, adjust lemon juice and maple syrup to taste.
5. Pour the filling onto the crust and spread evenly. Place into the refrigerator and chill for 2 hours. Enjoy!

Peanut Butter Caramel Rice Krispies

Cooking time: 20 minutes

Servings: 6-8

Ingredients

- 1 1/3 cups creamy peanut butter
- 6 cups rice crisp cereal
- 3/4 cup brown rice syrup
- 1 teaspoon vanilla extract
- 1/4 cup maple syrup

  Peanut butter drizzle:

- 1 teaspoon maple syrup
- 2 tablespoons creamy peanut butter
- 2 teaspoons water

Instructions

1. Line a baking pan with parchment paper.

2. To a cooking pot, add the maple syrup along with brown rice syrup and place on a medium heat. Bring to a boil, stir well and cook for a minute. Remove from the heat and add the peanut butter into the pot along with vanilla, stir until smooth.

3. Add the liquid to a bowl and then stir in rice crisp cereal until well combined.

4. Scoop the combined mixture into the prepared pan and spread evenly. Press down the mixture with a spatula and then place into the freezer for at least 10 minutes.

5. Meanwhile prepare the peanut butter drizzle. Mix the maple syrup together with the peanut butter in a different microwavable bowl, and then place the bowl in the microwave for 30 seconds to warm slightly. When done, add a tablespoon of water and then mix well until the mixture is smooth.

6. Carefully remove the krispies from the freezer, and then generously drizzle with the peanut butter and return back to the freezer for at least 10 minutes. When done, slice the krispies into squares and serve. Enjoy!

Vanilla Macaroons

Cooking time: 25 minutes

Servings: 6-8

Ingredients

- 1 cup almond milk
- 4 tablespoons raw cane sugar
- 1 tablespoon coconut flour
- 1 teaspoon vanilla extract
- 2 cups coconut, shredded
- 1 tablespoon almond flour

Instructions

1. Preheat the oven to 350F and then line a baking sheet with parchment paper.

2. Whisk the coconut milk together with the sweetener in a saucepan placed over medium heat but do not bring to a boil. When done, add the flours into the saucepan and stir the mixture well until combined and no clumps are left.

3. Increase the heat to high and allow the mixture to boil for 3 minutes, until thick, and then remove from heat.

4. Add the shredded coconut along with the vanilla to the mixture. Then measure 1 tablespoon of the mixture and place on the lined baking sheet. Bake for 13-15 minutes, until nicely browned.

5. When baked through, let cool and then serve. Enjoy!

Carrot Cake

Cooking time: 1 hour 20 minutes
Servings: 8

Ingredients

- 1 cup brown sugar
- 1 cup granulated sugar
- 1 teaspoon vanilla extract
- 2 cups baking flour
- 1 cup walnuts, chopped
- 1/2 teaspoon salt

- 1 1/4 cups apple sauce
- 1/4 teaspoon nutmeg
- 2 teaspoons baking powder
- 1 1/2 teaspoons ground cinnamon
- 1/2 teaspoon ginger
- 1 cup vegetable oil
- 3 cups carrots, grated
- 2 teaspoons baking soda
- 1 cup coconut, shredded

  Cream Cheese Frosting:
- 5 cups powdered sugar
- 8 oz vegan cream cheese, at room temperature
- 1 teaspoon vanilla extract
- 1/2 cup vegan butter, at room temperature

Instructions

1. Preheat the oven to 350F and then line a cake pan with a parchment paper. Then spray the pan bottom and sides with oil and set aside.
2. Mix the baking flour together with the baking powder, spices, salt and soda in a bowl, and then combine oil, brown and white sugars, vanilla extract, apple sauce in a separate bowl. Mix the carrots along with coconut in the bowl with apple sauce mixture.
3. Combine the dry ingredients with the wet ingredients. Then fold the batter into the walnuts.

4. Add the cake batter to the previously prepared mixture and then bake for at least an hour until baked through.

5. Transfer the cake from the oven to the refrigerator in order to cool completely until it can be easily removed from the pan.

6. When done, flip the cake upside down and then cut it into 2-3 layers.

7. Prepare the cheese frosting. Add the vegan cream cheese and vegan butter to a mixer and beat them together until well combined, and then add the vanilla extract and combine well.

8. Add a cup of powdered sugar bit by bit and process slowly. Process until smooth and creamy.

9. Assemble the cake by scooping 1 ½ cups of the prepared frosting on the bottom layer of the prepared cake, smoothen with a spatula and then add another layer of the cake. You can add another layer if desired.

10. When done, sprinkle the coconut or toasted almonds on the top layer of the cake, and then place the cake into the refrigerator until ready. Enjoy!

Pumpkin Pie

Cooking time: 45 minutes

Servings: 8

Ingredients

For the Pie Crust:

- 5 tablespoons butter
- 3 tablespoons ice water
- 1 1/4 cups flour
- 1/4 cup solid coconut oil
- 1/2 teaspoon salt

- 1 teaspoon sugar

For the Pumpkin Pie Filling:

- 1/4 cup brown sugar
- 15 oz. pumpkin puree
- 1 teaspoon ground cinnamon
- 2 tablespoons cornstarch
- 1/2 teaspoon ginger
- 1/2 teaspoon salt
- 1/8 teaspoon nutmeg
- 1/2 cup white sugar
- 1/8 teaspoon allspice
- 8 oz. firm tofu, silken
- 1 teaspoon vanilla extract
- 1/4 teaspoon cloves

Instructions

1. Prepare the pie crust. Spray the cooking pan generously with cooking spray and set aside.
2. Add flour, salt and sugar to a bowl, and then chop the butter and coconut oil into bite-size pieces, and then add to the bowl. Add the coconut oil and butter pieces to the flour and mix well with a pastry cutter or a fork.
3. Add a tablespoon of water to the flour mixture and knead the dough well until smooth and tough.
4. Then wrap the prepared dough in a plastic wrap and place into the refrigerator for 30 minutes until firm. Roll out the

dough on a floured parchment paper and press into the bottom of the pie pan.

5. Preheat the oven to 350F.

6. Add all the pumpkin pie filling ingredients to the blender and process until smooth. Add the blended filling onto the pie crust and use a spatula to spread evenly. Bake for 45 minutes, until the pie crust is nicely browned.

7. Remove the pumpkin pie from the oven and bring to a room temperature. Refrigerate for at least 4 hours and then serve with the whipped coconut cream. Enjoy!

Chapter 6: Drinks

Gingerbread Latte

Cooking time: 10 minutes

Servings:

Ingredients

- 1 tablespoon ginger, minced
- 1/2 cup espresso coffee
- 1 tablespoon sugar

- 1/2 teaspoon gingerbread spice
- 1 ½ cups coconut milk, frothed
- Whipped coconut cream

Instructions

1. Add ginger to a saucepan along with coffee, sugar and gingerbread spice, and bring to a boil over medium heat, and then simmer for at least 2 minutes.
2. When done, mix the add milk to the saucepan. Heat the mixture but do not bring to a boil.
3. Strain the drink and pour into the cups, and then add the coconut cream and sprinkle with the gingerbread spice. Enjoy!

Black Forest Shake

Cooking time: 15 minutes

Servings: 2

Ingredients

For Cherry Compote:

- 1 tablespoon sugar
- 2 tablespoons water
- Salt, to taste
- 1 cup cherries
- 2 teaspoons lime juice

For Vanilla Layer:

- 1 tablespoon sugar or sweetener

- 1/2 cup coconut milk ice cubes
- Vanilla extract, to taste
- 1/2 cup vanilla ice cream

  For Chocolate Layer:
- 1/2 cup vegan chocolate ice cream
- 2 tablespoons cherry compote
- 1/2 cup coconut milk or almond milk ice cubes
- 1 tablespoon cocoa powder
- 1 tablespoon sugar or sweetener

Instructions

1. Prepare cherry compote. Add all the compote ingredients to the skillet placed over medium heat, and cook until the liquid has slightly thickened and the cherries have softened. When done, let cool.
2. Add all the vanilla shake ingredients to a blender and process until smooth. Adjust the sweetness if needed and then scoop the mixture into the serving glasses.
3. Add the chocolate layer ingredients to the same blender along with 2 tablespoons of cherry compote, and then process until smooth.
4. Reserve some cherries for serving, and then spoon the cherry compote on top of the vanilla layer, and scoop the chocolate layer on top. Top with the reserved cherries and serve. Enjoy!

Turmeric Lassi

Cooking time: 10 minutes

Servings: 2

Ingredients

- 1 cup plain yogurt
- ½ teaspoon cayenne
- 1 cup almond milk or coconut milk, frozen into cubes
- 1 teaspoon turmeric
- 1 tablespoon sweetener
- 1 teaspoon ginger, candied, or 1/2 teaspoon fresh ginger, peeled
- Salt and pepper, to taste
- Coconut cream, whipped, for topping

Instructions

1. Add all the ingredients to a blender. Blitz until combined and smooth.
2. Pour into chilled glasses and garnish with turmeric and pepper or top the glasses with coconut cream. Enjoy!

Pumpkin Spice Turmeric Latte

Cooking time: 10 minutes

Servings: 2

Ingredients

- 1/4 cup water
- 1 ½ cups almond milk
- 1/2 teaspoon pumpkin pie spice
- 1 ½ tablespoons sweetener
- 1/2 teaspoon turmeric
- turmeric pumpkin pie spice or cinnamon, for garnish
- black pepper, to taste

Instructions

1. Add water and the spices to a pan and bring to a boil and then simmer for 1 minute.
2. Add almond milk a blender along with sweetener and process until frothy, and then add the frothy milk into the boiling water.
3. Bring to a light boil and then pour into the mugs. Sprinkle with pumpkin pie spice and the turmeric. Enjoy!

Mexican Hot Chocolate

Cooking time: 10 minutes
Servings: 3

Ingredients

- 6 cups plain or vanilla milk
- 2 teaspoons cinnamon
- 6 oz. vegan chocolate, or 6 tablespoons cocoa powder
- 3/4 teaspoon ground nutmeg
- 1 teaspoon vanilla extract
- Cayenne, to taste
- 1/3 cup maple syrup, or coconut, or pure cane sugar

Instructions

1. To a pot, add all the ingredients and cook for about 10 minutes over medium heat until all chocolate is melted. Then reduce the heat to low and close the lid. Cook for 1-2 minutes more.
2. When ready, scoop into the serving mugs and dust slightly with cocoa powder or top with the whipped coconut cream.

Coconut Cream Shake

Cooking time: 5 minutes

Servings: 2

Ingredients

- 2 teaspoons matcha
- 1 large banana, frozen
- 1 cup coconut milk
- ¼ cup ice cubes

Instructions

1. Add all the cream shake ingredients to a blender. Blitz until creamy and smooth.
2. Pour into chilled glasses and serve with your desired toppings. Enjoy!

Lemon Ginger Detox Tea

Cooking time: 5 minutes

Servings: 2

Ingredients

- 1/2 large lemon, squeezed
- 1 ¾ cups water
- 1 small ginger knob, peeled, sliced
- Cayenne, to taste
- 1/4 teaspoon sweetener

Instructions

1. Boil water and then pour it into a cup. Add ginger and let rest for a few minutes and then add cayenne along with the lemon juice and sweetener.
2. Stir the mixture well and serve. Enjoy!

Carrot Pineapple Ginger Juice

Cooking time: 5 minutes

Servings: 2

Ingredients

- 1 small ginger knob
- 1/4 pineapple, fresh
- 9 carrots

Instructions

1. Add all the ingredients to a juicer and juice well.
2. Stir well to combine. Pour into chilled glasses and serve.

Strawberry Shrub Mocktail

Cooking time: 5 minutes
Servings: 2

Ingredients

- ¾ oz. strawberry shrub
- 2 fresh basil leaves
- 2 strawberries
- 1 strip lemon zest
- 5 oz. plain seltzer, cold
- 3 ice cubes

Instructions

1. Add basil leaves to a jar along with lemon zest and strawberries, and then mash well until fragrant.
2. Add the ice and strawberry shrub into the jar mixture and then close the lid. Shake the mixture well for 30 seconds until cold and then strain the mixture into the champagne flute.
3. When done, top with seltzer and enjoy!

Cooking time: 10 minutes

Servings: 2

INGREDIENTS

- ½ cup water
- ⅛ teaspoon salt
- ¼ cup lime juice
- ¼ cup light blue agave nectar
- 16 oz. strawberries, frozen
- Lime slices, for garnish

INSTRUCTIONS

1. Add all the ingredients except lime slices to a blender. Blitz until combined and smooth.
2. Pour into chilled glasses and garnish with the lime slices. Enjoy!

Fresh Mint Julep

Cooking time: 15 minutes

Servings: 2

Ingredients

- 1 cup water
- ½ cup sugar
- ½ cup sugar snap peas, trimmed, halved
- 1 cup fresh mint leaves
- 1 ½ cups bourbon
- 1 cup pea greens, chopped
- 8 cups ice cubes
- ⅓ cup lemon juice
- Salt, to taste
- Pea blossoms, for garnish

Instructions

1. Add sugar along with a half cup of water to a saucepan and then bring to a boil. Turn the heat off and stir in the pea greens, and then let rest for about 25 minutes. Then strain the syrup into a bowl and refrigerate for about 30 minutes until cold.

2. Pour the remaining cup of water into a blender along with snap peas and blend for a minute, and then pour into a bowl through a sieve. Refrigerate for about 30 minutes until cold.

3. Prepare the cocktails. Add 2 tablespoons of mint to a glass along with 1 ½ tablespoons of the prepared syrup, and then mash the mint. When done, pour 2 teaspoons of lemon juice to the glass along with a tablespoon of pea juice and 3 tablespoons of the bourbon, and then add a half cup of the ice cubes and stir well. Garnish with mint, pea blossoms and extra pea greens. Serve and enjoy!

BONUS!!!!

The Best 30-Day Meal Plan

The Best 30-Day Meal Plan

30-Days Meal Plan

Day 1
Breakfast: Cardamom Peach Quinoa Porridge

Lunch: Banh Mi

Snack: Oatmeal Bars

Dinner: Brown Rice Stir Fry with Vegetables

Day 2
Breakfast: Chia Berries Smoothie

Lunch: Sweet Potato Buddha Bowl Almond Butter Dressing

Dessert: Vegan Brownies

Dinner: Grilled Veggie Skewers

Day 3
Breakfast: Vegan Breakfast Sandwich

Lunch: Curry Spiced Sweet Potato Wild Rice Burgers

Snack: Coconut Bacon

Dinner: Eggplant Teriyaki Bowls

Day 4
Breakfast: Tofu Detox Smoothie

Lunch: Calabacitas Quesadillas

Dessert: Vegan Chocolate

Dinner: Lentil Shepherd's Pie

Day 5
Breakfast: Greek Chickpeas Toast

Lunch: Chickpea Avocado Salad Sandwich With Cranberries

Snack: Spiced Applesauce

Dinner: Quinoa and Black Bean Chilli

Day 6
Breakfast: Tofu Pancakes

Lunch: Rice Paper Rolls With Mango And Mint

Dessert: Peanut Butter Cup Cookies

Dinner: Mac And Cheese

Day 7
Breakfast: Waffles with Blueberry Sauce

Lunch: Turmeric Chickpea Salad Sandwich

Snack: Spinach and Artichoke Dip

Dinner: Butternut Squash Linguine With Fried Sage

Breakfast: Maple Blueberry Shake

Lunch: Mexican Quinoa

Dessert: Lemon Tarts

Dinner: Paella

Breakfast: Cucumber Avocado Smoothie

Lunch: Potato Fritters

Snack: Wheat Thins

Dinner: Spicy Thai Peanut Sauce Over Roasted Sweet Potatoes And Rice

Breakfast: Blueberry Oatmeal Waffles

Lunch: Tempeh Reuben

Dessert: Peanut Butter Caramel Rice Krispies

Dinner: Butternut Squash Chipotle Chili With Avocado

Day 11
Breakfast: Jam Cheese Sandwich

Lunch: Broccoli Pesto With Pasta And Cherry Tomatoes

Snack: Baked Sweet Potato Fries

Dinner: Chickpea Biryani

Day 12
Breakfast: Valentine Smoothie

Lunch: Broccoli Pesto With Pasta And Cherry Tomatoes

Dessert: Vanilla Macaroons

Dinner: Chinese Eggplant

Day 13
Breakfast: Waffles with Blueberry Sauce

Lunch: Korean Barbecue Tempeh Wraps

Dessert: Carrot Cake

Dinner: Black Pepper Tofu With Bok Choy

Day 14
Breakfast: Pina Colada Smoothie

Lunch: Crab Cakes

Dessert: Carrot Cake

Dinner: Spaghetti Alla Puttanesca

Day 15
Breakfast: Cardamom Peach Quinoa Porridge

Lunch: Smoky Black Beans Parsley Chimichurri

Snack: Cornmeal Breaded Tofu

Dinner: Thai Red Curry

Day 16
Breakfast: Maca Caramel Smoothie

Lunch: Tuna Sandwich With Chickpeas

Dessert: Pumpkin Pie

Dinner: Thai Green Curry With Spring Vegetables

Day 17

Breakfast: Greek Chickpeas Toast

Lunch: Sweet Potato Toast

Snack: Tofu Fish Sticks

Dinner: Tamarind Potato Curry

Day 18

Breakfast: Tofu Pancakes

Lunch: Chickpeas with Dates, Turmeric, Cinnamon and Almonds

Dessert: Vegan Brownies

Dinner: West African Stew With Sweet Potato And Greens

Day 19

Breakfast: Blueberry Oatmeal Waffles

Lunch: Cucumber Avocado Toast

Snack: Spinach and Artichoke Dip

Dinner: Eggplant and Sesame Stir Fry

Day 20

Breakfast: Chia Berries Smoothie

Lunch: Moroccan Veggie Soup

Dessert: Peanut Butter Cup Cookies

Dinner: Kale Slaw

Day 21

Breakfast: Jam Cheese Sandwich

Lunch: Tofu Salad With Sesame Dressing

Dessert: Vegan Brownies

Dinner: Grilled Veggie Skewers

Day 22

Breakfast: Chia Berries Smoothie

Lunch: Sweet Potato Buddha Bowl Almond Butter Dressing

Snack: Oatmeal Bars

Dinner: Brown Rice Stir Fry with Vegetables

Day 23

Breakfast: Valentine Smoothie

Lunch: Thai Red Curry Butternut Squash Soup

Dessert: Lemon Tarts

Dinner: Grilled Veggie Skewers

Day 24
Breakfast: Vegan Breakfast Sandwich

Lunch: Tex Mex Black Bean And Avocado Salad

Snack: Spiced Applesauce

Dinner: Eggplant Teriyaki Bowls

Day 25
Breakfast: Greek Chickpeas Toast

Lunch: Lentil Fattoush Salad

Dessert: Peanut Butter Caramel Rice Krispies

Dinner: Lentil Shepherd's Pie

Day 26
Breakfast: Tofu Detox Smoothie

Lunch: Sweet Potato Salad

Snack: Wheat Thins

Dinner: Quinoa and Black Bean Chilli

Breakfast: Maple Blueberry Shake

Lunch: Lentil Salad With Spinach And Pomegranate

Snack: Baked Sweet Potato Fries

Dinner: Butternut Squash Linguine With Fried Sage

Breakfast: Waffles with Blueberry Sauce

Lunch: Caesar Salad Recipe Creamy Caesar Dressing

Dessert: Vanilla Macaroons

Dinner: Mac And Cheese

Breakfast: Cardamom Peach Quinoa Porridge

Lunch: Broccoli Salad Curry Dressing

Snack: Cornmeal Breaded Tofu

Dinner: Paella

Breakfast: Jam Cheese Sandwich

Lunch: Carrot Ginger Soup

Dessert: Pumpkin Pie

Dinner: Spicy Thai Peanut Sauce Over Roasted Sweet Potatoes And Rice

Conclusion

Here is the end of your journey with the Plant Based Diet.

The Plant Based diet is suitable for anyone who wants to improve the quality of everyday life, boost the level of your energy, make the health better and to prevent various diseases.

Usually people decide to go with Plant Based diet due to one or several reasons. People might switch to Plant Based diet due to their ethical reasons, as they believe all live creatures have a right to live, be free, and fairly treated. You can find your own reasons.

There are many sources of healthy nutrients in plant based products. So, you don't have to worry about getting enough vitamins to your body. This book will help you to make healthy vegan Meal Plan for the whole family and spend less time in the kitchen.

Remember that Plant Based is not only about the diet, but about changing your lifestyle to a more healthy and balanced one.

CPSIA information can be obtained
at www.ICGtesting.com
Printed in the USA
BVHW050724280721
613018BV00009B/247